The Twentieth

by Cindy Barden

illustrated by
Corbin Hillam

Author
Cindy Barden

Illustrator
Corbin Hillam

Cover Illustration and Select Transparencies
Art Kirchhoff

Photo Credits: The Dust Bowl 1936–1940
Library of Congress Prints & Photographs Division, FSA-OWI Collection
"Migrant Mother" 1936 Reproduction Number: USZ62-95653
Oklahoma dust bowl refugees, 1935 Reproduction Number: LC-USZ62-56051 DLC
Son of farmer in dust bowl area, 1936 Reproduction Number: LC-USZ62-130123 DLC
Winds of the dust bowl, Reproduction Number: LC-USZ62-129049 DLC

Book Design and Production
Good Neighbor Press, Inc.

Table of Contents

Activities marked with an * can be used with one of the transparencies at the back of the book.

Activities

Teaching Guide for Transparency Pages

Fashions of the Roaring Twenties

During the Roaring Twenties, young women called "flappers" "bobbed" their hair and began dressing in ways that outraged their parents. Previously, women's dresses covered them completely from neck to ankles. Suddenly, fashions changed. Necklines plunged and hemlines rose above the knees.

Although young people flaunted the extremes of fashions, the hemlines for most women's dresses came about halfway between the ankle and knee. No women or girls wore pants or shorts, even at home.

Men's clothing was a bit more conservative in the 1920s. Trousers widened to as much as 24 inches at the bottoms. Raccoon coats were very popular with college men. Boys wore knickers, suspenders, and bow ties.

From Horse and Buggy to Outer Space

At the beginning of the century, airplanes were only dreams and cars were considered "rich men's toys"—smelly contraptions that would never replace the reliable horse and buggy. Advances in technology during the twentieth century enabled people to travel farther and faster than anyone in 1900 could have dreamed possible.

As the century progressed, automobiles became more affordable, diesel locomotives replaced steam-powered engines, small bi-planes gave way to supersonic jets that traveled faster than the speed of sound, and space shuttles took people to the moon.

My How Things Have Changed!

Students can use these tables to make comparisons, create graphs, and begin discussions on changes in the twentieth century. Explain the meaning of population density. Students can compare the population density of their state to the average for the U.S.

Ask students to explain why even though the total population increased between the 1950 and 1960 census, the number of people per square mile decreased. (Alaska became a state in 1959, adding a great deal of area, but few people.)

The Dust Bowl

The economic problems that began with the stock market crash of 1929 continued to worsen as drought struck the U.S. A large area in the southern part of the Great Plains region became known as the Dust Bowl during the 1930s.

To compound the problem, the winds began blowing almost continuously in 1936. Huge clouds of dust moved across the prairie, in some cases darkening the sky all the way to the Atlantic Ocean.

People slept with wet cloths over their faces to filter out the dust. Animals were buried alive or choked to death on the dust.

People died if they remained outside too long during a dust storm. Many also died because of severe lung damage caused by breathing dust.

Three to four inches of topsoil blew away over the next four years, leaving only hard red clay. Farming became impossible.

When crops failed, farmers couldn't make mortgage payments on their farms. A thousand families a week lost their farms in Texas, Oklahoma, and Arkansas. Many migrated west in search of a better life.

World War II Advertising

Colorful posters published during World War II promoted patriotism by recruiting men for the Army and encouraging people to buy war bonds and plant Victory Gardens. Rosie the Riveter became the symbol of the working woman during World War II.

Teaching Guide for Transparency Pages

Toys of the Twentieth Century

Many toys introduced during the twentieth century have stood the test of time and remain popular today. Ask students how many they recognize. Ask them to write or tell about their favorite toys. Discuss how toys have changed over the years.

Communications

The telephone and radio were novelties at the beginning of the twentieth century. By mid-century most Americans had a radio and telephone. Many owned a television set. As technology improved, electronics became smaller, more dependable, more sophisticated, and less expensive. The introduction of transistors, silicone chips, fiber optics, and communication satellites has made instantaneous communication possible around the world.

Ask students to identify each item shown on the transparency and discuss how that item changed people's ability to communicate.

Styles in the Sixties

Like the twenties, fashions in the sixties went to extremes, but this time for both men and women. Women's styles ranged from the conservative clothing, hats, and hairstyles worn by Jackie Kennedy, "First Lady of Fashion," to the non-style of the hippies. Men wore their hair longer in imitation of the Beatles and other rock stars. Beards and mustaches became more common.

By mid-decade, women wore miniskirts or hot pants and go-go boots. By the end of the decade, peasant skirts or granny dresses and chunky shoes had become popular. Hair styles were either very short and boyish or long and lanky.

Many styles, like bell-bottomed jeans, love beads, and t-shirts were worn by both men and women.

Men wore bright colors, double-breasted, patterned sports jackets and slacks, Nehru jackets, and turtlenecks. Ties, when worn, were up to five inches wide with wild patterns.

Ask students to compare sixties styles to styles shown on the Roaring Twenties transparency. Compare these styles to popular fashions today.

Name ____________________

Timeline 1900–1909

1900: U.S. population is 75,994,575.
L. Frank Baum published *The Wonderful World of Oz.*
Estimated total number of cars in the U.S. is 8,000.
Construction began on the first subway in New York City.
The Hawaiian Islands became a U.S. territory.

1901: President McKinley was assassinated: Roosevelt became president.
The first Nobel Peace Prize was awarded.

1901–1909 U.S. President Theodore Roosevelt.

1902: William Carrier invented the air conditioner.
New: Frank Fleer invented an early form of bubble gum called Blibber Blubber.

1903: Orville and Wilbur Wright made the first successful airplane flight.
Jack London published *Call of the Wild.*
First World Series game played.
The U.S. began digging the Panama Canal.
New: teddy bears.

1904: U.S. Supreme Court denied blacks the right to vote.
Carry Nation began a hatchet-carrying crusade against liquor.
Mary McLeod Bethune opened the first Negro Girls School.
The ice cream cone was invented at the St. Louis World's Fair.

1905: First nickelodeon opened in Pittsburgh.
Football was so rough President Roosevelt wanted to ban it.

1906: U.S. Senate passed the Food and Drug Act.
An earthquake in San Francisco killed more than 700 people.
Oklahoma became the 46th state.

1908: Henry Ford introduced the Model T. The price was $850.

1909: Robert Peary and Matthew Henson are the first to reach North Pole.

1909–1913 U.S. President William Taft.

1. Use a reference source. What two bodies of water did the Panama Canal connect? Why was that important?

____

____

2. Read the list of important events that took place between 1900 and 1910. Which event do you think has had the greatest influence on people's lives? Give reasons for your answer.

____

____

____

Name ________________________________

Life Was Different Then

People began the twentieth century with a sense of optimism, peace, and prosperity. Industrialization allowed factories to mass-produce goods, reducing prices to an all-time low.

If you had been alive in 1900, you probably would have lived on a farm or in a small town. That's where most Americans lived. You wouldn't have had a radio, television, computer, or microwave. Since only about 2% of Americans had a telephone, you might not have been one of the lucky ones. Chances are you wouldn't travel in a plane. Most people during this decade never saw an airplane.

You might have had a chance to go to a movie, but it would have been a "silent" film in black and white. The good news: a movie ticket only cost a nickel. The first nickelodeon (nickel theater) opened in Pittsburgh in 1905. Three years later there were 10,000 operating in the U.S.

Not too many people owned cars yet, but they were becoming more and more popular. Concerned with the dangers of speeding, 15 states had speed limits of 20 miles per hour by 1906. The first cross country auto trip took 52 days.

Life expectancy was much lower at the beginning of the twentieth century: 47.3 years for white women; 46.3 years for white men; and 33.0 years for blacks.

Women had few rights in the early 1900s. In an article published in the *Ladies Home Journal*, former president Grover Cleveland stated that "No sensible and responsible woman wants to vote."

The original formula for Coca-Cola was changed in 1903 when caffeine was substituted for cocaine.

May Sutton caused an uproar at the Wimbledon Championship Tournament when she appeared in a tennis dress two inches above her ankles. Officials gave her an ultimatum: lower the hem or be disqualified.

For fun, people spent time at family get-togethers, baseball games, and picnics. They took long Sunday drives in their horse and buggy (or new family car). They gathered around the piano for a sing-along or played a new game: ping pong. Lucky children might have owned one of the hot toys of the decade: a teddy bear.

1. The annual pay for teachers during this decade was $325. What does annual mean? ________

   ____

2. The average wage during the decade was $12.98 per week for 59 hours of work. At that rate, how much would a person earn for working 52 weeks? ________________

   ____

3. At that rate, what was the average hourly rate? ________________

Name ______________________________

Timeline 1910–1919

1910: U.S. population is 91,972,266.
Estimated number of cars in the U.S. is 458,500.
First electric toaster available.
Boy Scouts of America began.
New: Dr. Pepper.

1911: Fingerprints first used to solve a crime.

1912: The luxury liner Titanic sank, killing 1,513.
Juliette Low founded the Girl Scouts.
New Mexico became the 47th state.
Arizona became the 48th state.
Alaska became a U.S. territory.
New: Life Saver candy for 5 cents a roll.

1913–1921 U.S. President: Woodrow Wilson.

1913: The first drive-in gas station opened in Pittsburgh.
Toys first added to boxes of Cracker Jacks.
Assembly line production reduced cost of Model T to $260.
New: zippers; Erector Sets; Tinker Toys.

1914: The Panama canal opened.
World War I began in Europe.
Mother's Day became an official holiday.
First national income tax: average payment $41.

1915: The millionth Model T, which sold for $345, rolled off the assembly line.
Alexander Graham Bell made first transcontinental call from New York to San Francisco.
New: Bayer aspirin.

1916: Jeannette Rankin (Montana): first woman elected to Congress.
Congress passed a Child Labor law making it illegal for children under 16 to work in mines and factories and limited work to eight hours a day, 48 hours a week.
New: Lincoln Logs

1917: The U.S. declared War on Germany; entered World War I.
Puerto Rico became a U.S. territory.
New: SOS pads.

1918: World War I ended.
By the end of 1918, there were 6.2 million cars in the U.S.

1919: Eighteenth Amendment prohibited sale of liquor.
About one-third of American homes had electricity.

1. Use a reference source. In what year did Alexander Graham Bell invent the telephone? ______

2. Use a dictionary. Define *transcontinental.* ______________________________

____

3. The average cost of a gallon of milk during this decade was 32 cents.

   What does a gallon of milk cost today?______________________

Name ______________________________

The War to End All Wars

When the U.S. entered World War I, people believed this global conflict would be the "war to end all wars." It became a war of immense armies fought with tanks, airplanes, submarines, and poison gas.

Great changes occurred in the 1910s as the U.S. became an industrial leader. Many issues we face today became important including immigration, poverty, Civil Rights, labor unions, and working conditions. The national debt rose to $1.15 billion.

The U.S. remained mainly a nation of farms and small towns, but changes were beginning. More people moved into cities to work in factories. Many factory owners wanted to make as much money as possible by paying workers as little as possible. Working conditions were unsafe and unhealthy.

A fire in a New York dressmaking factory in 1911 killed 141 women and brought unsafe working conditions in many industries to public attention. Labor unions flourished.

Not only did adults work long hours in terrible conditions, in some areas, poor children as young as 12 worked 12 to 14 hours a day in factories and mines.

The day after Henry Ford announced a raise for automotive workers to $5 a day in 1914, 12,000 workers applied for jobs. The average wage for skilled workers then was $2 a day!

Mass production of the Model T made cars so affordable they no longer were "rich men's toys." Chevrolet, DeSoto, Dodge, and Nash were all introduced during the 1910s. Prestige cars were Cadillacs, Buicks, Pierce Arrows, Haynes, Packards, and Studebakers.

Air mail service began in 1918. The plane was due to take off from a park in Washington, D.C. in front of thousands of spectators. However, the pilot couldn't get the plane started. Finally he discovered the tank was empty. After take-off, the pilot was so flustered, he flew southeast instead of north to Philadelphia. When he made an emergency landing to get directions, the propeller broke. A truck finally arrived to deliver the mail.

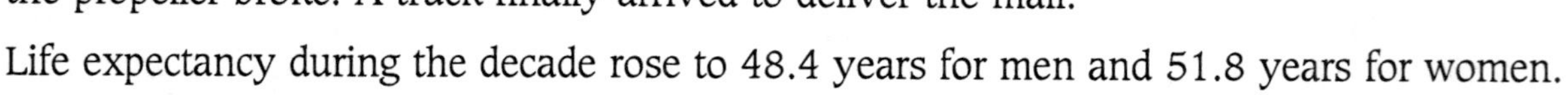

Life expectancy during the decade rose to 48.4 years for men and 51.8 years for women.

1. Write your answer on another sheet of paper. How would you feel about not attending school and working 60 or more hours a week to help support your family?

2. Women became active in the Suffrage Movement. Use a reference source. What did the Suffrage Movement hope to obtain for women?

____

Name ____

Timeline 1920–1929

1920: U.S. population is 105,710,620.
Nineteenth Amendment granted women the right to vote.
First U.S. cross-country airmail flight.
Less than 15% of people in the U.S. had a telephone.
The National Negro Baseball League organized.
New: pogo sticks.

1921–1923 U.S. President: William G. Harding.

1921: 16-year-old Margaret Gorman: first Miss America.
First skywriting.
New: Band-Aids; Wrigley's gum.

1922: Henry Berliner made the first helicopter flight.
The Lincoln Memorial was dedicated in Washington, D.C.
New: Eskimo Pies; "Readers Digest."

1923–1929 U.S. President: Calvin Coolidge.

1923: Yankee Stadium opened.
New: Welch's grape jelly; "Time" magazine.

1924: First Disney cartoon: "Alice's Wonderland."
Model T cost $290.
New: Wheaties; Kleenex tissue; crossword puzzle books.

1925: Warner Brothers began experimenting with "talkies."
Goodyear blimp began sky advertising.
Unemployment rate: 3%.
Movies cost 10 cents.

1926: Book-of-the-Month-Club began.
First radio jingle broadcast (Wheaties).

1927: Charles A. Lindbergh made the first solo nonstop flight across the Atlantic Ocean.
The Ford Motor Company discontinued the Model T and replaced it with the more modern Model A which sold for $395. Henry Ford announced, "a customer could have the car in any color as long as it was black."

1928: First Disney cartoon with sound: "Steamboat Willie."
First three homes in U.S. had television sets.
Billboard Magazine published first music charts.

1929: Stock Market Crash: Great Depression began.
Experiments began with color television.
First Academy Awards presented.
Over 23,000,000 cars in the U.S.
First color movie with sound.
New: Rice Krispies; Duncan yo yo's.

1929–1933 U.S. President: Herbert Hoover.

1. What does it cost to go to a movie today? __________

2. Which new products mentioned do people still use today?

____

MP4826

Name ____________________

The Roar Before the Crash

Most Americans in the 1920s hoped to put thoughts of war behind them. They wanted to put the new inventions in communications, transportation, and technology to peaceful uses and expected an era of world peace and prosperity.

The 1920s began an era of freedom for women who finally had the right to vote. They wore "scandalous" hairstyles and fashions.

Beginning in 1923, dance marathons became the rage.

During the twenties, higher wages and new products tempted people to spend money freely. Average annual earnings rose to $1236. People began to buy on credit. Stock prices climbed and people invested heavily. They even mortgaged their homes and borrowed money to buy stocks. Economists predicted prosperity.

Electricity was so new in the 1920s that many people feared it. They bought special caps to cover electrical outlets so the electricity couldn't spill out into the room.

Although the decade began with the hope of lasting prosperity, hopes shattered with the Stock Market Crash of 1929 and panic broke out. Between Black Thursday (October 24, 1929) and Terrible Tuesday (October 29, 1929) so many shares of stock were sold that the market collapsed. In one day stock values dropped between $10 billion and $15 billion. Even those who hadn't invested in the Stock Market were ruined when banks went broke.

1. Use reference sources. What was a dance marathon? Would you like to participate in a dance marathon? Why or why not?

   ____

2. Ask an adult: What does "mortgaged their homes" mean? ____________________

   ____

3. The illiteracy rate reached a new low of 6% of the population. Use a reference source. What does illiteracy mean?

   ____

   ____

4. Use reference sources. Describe the Harlem Renaissance. ____________________

   ____

   ____

5. Describe how you think you would have felt if your family suddenly went from rich to poor.

   ____

   ____

Name ______________________________

What Do You Think?

For decades, many people had tried to make alcohol illegal in the U.S. They blamed alcohol for the rising rate in divorces, family problems, crimes, violence, and poverty. They claimed the grain used to make alcohol could be better used for food.

The Eighteenth Amendment made the manufacture, sale, import, and export of liquor illegal in the U.S, but the government had too little money and too few people to enforce this unpopular law. Although all taverns were officially closed, illegal nightclubs sprang up everywhere. People smuggled liquor from other countries and produced it in illegal factories.

No other law was so violently opposed and ignored at all levels of American society. As a result, many people felt Prohibition promoted disrespect for the law.

People tried to repeal Prohibition as soon as it was passed. They claimed the law was an invasion of people's private lives. Others felt prohibition encouraged organized crime and promoted corruption at almost every level of government.

In the 1920s Utah lawmakers tried to make it illegal for women to wear "skirts higher than three inches above the ankle."

1. What do you think about the illegalization of alcohol? ______________________________

2. Do you think the government has the right to ban the sale of alcohol, tobacco, drugs, or any other items? Why or why not?

3. Why do you think people were so violently opposed to prohibition? ______________________________

4. Do you think there are some things the government should not attempt to regulate?

5. Do you think the government has the right to say what people can or cannot wear in public?

   Why or why not? ______________________________

MP4826

Name ____

Timeline 1930–1939

1930: U.S. population is 122,775,046.
Over 1,300 banks went broke.
"Elm Farm Ollie" became first cow to fly in an airplane.
Pluto was discovered.
New: Nancy Drew mysteries.

1931: "Star-Spangled Banner" became the national anthem.
The Empire State Building opened.
2,300 banks failed.
New: Scotch Tape; electric razors; Scrabble; Alka-Seltzer.

1932: Lindbergh baby kidnapped.
First U.S. winter Olympics held at Lake Placid, NY.
Cost of mailing a letter rose to three cents.
First federal tax on gasoline: one cent per gallon.
Amelia Earhart: first woman to fly solo across the Atlantic.
Unemployment rate: 25% (13,000,000 people).

1933–1945 U.S. President: Franklin D. Roosevelt.

1933: Adolf Hitler became the leader of Nazi Germany.
Japan, Germany, and Italy signed treaty of alliance.
Twenty-First Amendment repealed Prohibition.
Frances Perkins became Secretary of Labor: first woman named to a presidential cabinet.
New: Mickey Mouse watches; comic books; drive-in movies.

1934: Fifty percent of the homes in the U.S. had radios.
Donald Duck first appeared in a cartoon.

1935: Social Security Act signed.
New: parking meters; paperback books; electric typewriters; Monopoly game.

1936: ***New:*** electric guitars; "Life" magazine.
Olympics held in Berlin, Germany.

1937: Child labor law passed.
Golden Gate Bridge opened.
Chicago's Cook County Hospital: first blood bank to store blood from live donors.
New: "Look" magazine; Wheat Chex; electrical digital calculators.

1938: Germany annexed Austria.
Disney produced first full-length animated film, "Snow White and the Seven Dwarfs."
New: "Jack and Jill" magazine; saddle shoes; Superman comics; Scrabble.

1939: Germany annexed Czechoslovakia; invaded Poland.
Great Britain, France, Australia, New Zealand, and Canada declared war on Germany.
Television demonstrated at New York World's Fair.
About 80% of U.S. homes had radios.

1. Use the Internet. What is the current unemployment rate? ________________

2. Use reference sources. Add three more items to the Timeline. ____________________________

____

Name ______________________________

The Great Depression of the 1930s

The stock market crash of 1929 began a period of economic problems which lasted until the mid 1940s. The Great American Dream turned into a nightmare. The land of opportunity became the land of desperation. Hope and optimism turned to despair.

President Hoover assured people that the crisis was "a passing incident in our national lives." He believed relief help should come from churches and private organization, not the government.

As businesses, industries, and banks shut down, millions of people became unemployed and homeless. Schools closed in rural areas. Shanty towns nicknamed Hoovervilles sprang up in city dumps, vacant lots, and under bridges.

Many people relied on soup kitchens for food. They stood in bread lines to buy day-old bread. Men walked around with their pockets turned inside out to show they were broke. As more people lost jobs, they had less money to spend, so they bought fewer products. As a result, stores and factories needed fewer workers and more people lost their jobs.

Drought conditions in several states caused further problems. Between 1930 and 1935, 750,000 farms were lost through bankruptcy.

When Franklin D. Roosevelt took office in 1933, he urged Congress to quickly pass measures to relieve poverty, improve the economy, reduce unemployment, and stabilize the banking industry. The Civilian Conservation Corps (1933) provided jobs for needy young men in forests and national parks. The Works Progress Administration (1935) provided federal funding for jobs in construction of public buildings, slum clearance, flood control, and road maintenance. The WPA also provided jobs for artists (painting murals on public buildings), writers (conducting research projects), and actors and actresses (touring and performing in rural areas).

Roosevelt's programs didn't provide an immediate cure, but they did address basic needs and gave Americans new hope.

During the 1930s advances in technology, communications, and transportation continued at a much slower pace. Life expectancy rose to 58.1 years for men and 61.6 years for women. Milk cost 14 cents a quart; bread, 9 cents a loaf; and round steak, 42 cents a pound.

1. Use a dictionary. What is the economic meaning of depression? ______________________

   ____

2. Use a dictionary. Define *drought*. ______________________________

   ____

3. Use a reference source. How many times was Roosevelt elected President? ____________

Name ______________________________

Timeline 1940–1949

1940: U.S. population is 131,669,275.
Unemployment in U.S.: 8,120,000.
National debt: $43 billion.

1941: Germany took over Denmark, Norway, Netherlands, Belgium, and France; invaded the Soviet Union.
Nazis ordered Jews to wear yellow stars.
Japan attacked Pearl Harbor on December 7th.
The United States and Britain declared war on Japan.
New: nickel jukeboxes; Morton Salt; nylon; Jeeps.

1942: U.S. surrendered the Philippines to Japan.
Mass murder of millions of Jews began at Auschwitz.
Automobile production ceased because of the war.
Rubber tires were rationed.
Japanese-Americans were relocated to internment camps.

1943: Allies won in North Africa.
Italy surrendered.
Rationing of shoes, food, and other goods began in the U.S.
Batman became a comic strip hero.
Half the workers on assembly lines were women.
New: Chutes and Ladders.

1944: Allies invaded Normandy, France on June 6th.
Paris was liberated in August.
Allies won Battle of the Bulge in December.
The first eye bank was established at New York Hospital.
Anne Frank and family were arrested by the Gestapo in Holland.
New: "Seventeen" magazine.

1945–1953 U.S. President Harry S Truman.

1945: Allies liberated concentration camps.
U.S. regained control of the Philippines.
President Roosevelt died; Harry Truman became President.
Germany surrendered on May 7th.
U.S. dropped atomic bombs on Hiroshima and Nagasaki, Japan.
First successful digital computer, ENIAC, weighed 30 tons.

1946: ***New:*** bikini swimsuits.

1947: Jackie Robinson: first black player in the Major League.
Commercial television available with 13 stations.
Chuck Yeager: first pilot to break the sound barrier.
New: Slinky.

1949: ***New:*** Polaroid Land camera; Candyland; Clue; Silly Putty.

1. Use a dictionary. Define *internment.* ______________________________

2. Use a reference source. What was the Gestapo? ______________________________

3. Use a reference source. What does "break the sound barrier" mean? ______________________________

____

Name ______________________________

World War II Changed America

By the end of the thirties, the U.S. was slowly recovering from the economic problems that began in 1929. When the Japanese bombed Pearl Harbor in December 1941, the U.S. entered World War II. War production pulled the U.S. out of the Great Depression as factories began producing tanks, planes, ships, and other military equipment.

World War II affected people in many ways. Men went off to war. Millions of women took jobs outside the home for the first time. Several hundred thousand women enlisted in the military.

People were faced with restrictions on what and how much they could buy. War rationing affected the availability of cars, gasoline, appliances, food, clothing, and even children's toys.

The government encouraged people to plant "Victory Gardens"—small vegetable gardens to grow their own food. In 1943 Victory Gardens produced about one-third of all vegetables consumed in the U.S. Recycling became a way of life as the government held scrap drives for steel, tin, paper, rubber, and other items needed to help the war effort. Women donated silk dresses: the silk was used to make parachutes.

Cloth was rationed, so women's skirts became shorter and clothing less frilly. Many women who worked in factories began wearing slacks for the first time.

Radio became the lifeline for Americans in the 1940s, providing news, music, and entertainment. Programs included soap operas, quiz shows, children's hours, mystery stories, drama, and sports. The United States emerged from World War II as a world superpower, challenged only by the USSR.

The Marshall Plan helped war-torn countries in Europe rebuild and rejoin the world economy. The Soviet Union took advantage of the chaos in Europe to spread communism. Disputes over ideology with the USSR led to the Cold War.

By the end of the decade, 55% of U.S. homes had indoor plumbing. Life expectancy rose to 68.2 years for women and 60.8 years for men.

1. Use a dictionary. Define *rationing*. ______________________________

2. Use reference sources. What does U.S.S.R. stand for? ______________________________

   ____

3. List several ways people's daily lives were affected by World War II. ______________________________

   ____

   ____

Name ______________________________

Timeline 1950–1959

1950: U.S. population is 150,697,361.
First "Peanuts" comic strip published.
Smokey the Bear became the symbol for forest fire safety.
Senator Joseph McCarthy began anti-Communist crusade.
New: Yahtzee.

1950–1953: U.S. armed forces fought in Korea.

1952: The Immigration and Naturalization Act removed racial and ethnic barriers to becoming a U.S. citizen.
First atomic submarine launched.
New: Mr. Potato Head.

1953–1961 U.S. President Dwight D. Eisenhower.

1953: Dr. Jonas Salk developed a vaccine against polio.

1954: U.S. Supreme Court outlawed segregation in public schools.
New: Frozen TV dinners.

1955: Rosa Parks refused to give up her seat on a public bus in Montgomery, Alabama.
Montgomery bus boycott.
Disneyland opened in California.
Dr. Albert Sabin created an oral polio vaccine.
First MacDonald's opened.

1956: Work began on the interstate highway system.
Segregation on public transportation became illegal.
New: Playdoh.

1957: ***New:*** frozen pizza.

1958: **Explorer I:** first U.S. satellite orbited Earth.
New: hula hoop.

1959: Alaska and Hawaii became states.
The average car cost $1,180.
New: Barbie doll.
The most far-reaching change in communications came in television broadcasting. During the 1950s, television became the dominant mass media for news and entertainment. A 1950 survey reported that children 11 to 15 spent as much time watching TV as they did going to school. By the end of the decade, nearly 90% of American homes had televisions.
Life expectancy rose to 71.1 years for women and 65.6 years for men. The average annual salary during the decade was $2,992 and a loaf of bread cost 14 cents.

1. Use a dictionary. Define *segregation.* ______________________________

2. Use reference sources. What country launched the first satellite and what was it called?

   ____

3. Keep track of the number of hours you watch TV for one week. What is your average number of hours per day? ______________

Name ______________________________

The Fabulous Fifties

When World War II ended, thousands of young men returned home to resume their lives. They wanted to find jobs, get married, have children, and buy homes. American industry flourished by providing goods not available during the war, as well as items to meet the new American lifestyle. Cars and televisions became status symbols of prosperity. New highways provided the means to travel quickly from place to place. Shopping malls sprang up around the country.

Many women who had worked to meet the demands of industry during the war were satisfied to return to the traditional roles of mothers, wives, and homemakers. Other women missed their new-found freedom and independence.

The fifties became a time of optimism as more and more middle class Americans enjoyed "the good life." Before the country could completely recover from World War II, however, the Korean Conflict developed and U.S. servicemen went off to another war.

The decade also brought about a sense of national anxiety at the possibility of a third world war due to the increased tensions between the U.S. and the U.S.S.R. Fearing a nuclear attack, many Americans built fallout shelters as the world powers developed more powerful bombs.

Teenage boys with crew cuts or flat tops wore t-shirts and blue jeans. Girls in pony tails wore saddle shoes, white ankle socks, and poodle skirts made of felt and decorated with sequins and poodle appliques.

Rock 'n' roll, a combination of country-Western, rhythm-and-blues, and gospel music with a strong beat dominated the music of the fifties.

Popular TV shows of the fifties portrayed ideal families, schools, and neighborhoods. Top shows included "Lassie," "The Honeymooners," "Father Knows Best," "The Adventures of Ozzie and Harriet," "I Love Lucy," "Disneyland," "Leave It to Beaver," and "The Ed Sullivan Show."

1. Describe a current clothing or hair style fad and explain why you do or don't like it.

____

____

2. Have you ever heard rock 'n roll music? What do you think of it? ______________

____

____

3. Do you think most television shows today portray ideal or realistic situations?

____

____

____

Name ______________________________

Timeline 1960–1969

1960: U.S. population is 179,323,175.
New: Game of Life.
Average weekly salary: $89.72.

1961–1963 U.S. President John F. Kennedy.

1961: Peace Corps created.
New: Ken doll; Carousel slide projector.

1962: The U.S. State Department denied passports to American citizens who were members of the Communist Party.
Astronaut John Glenn: first American to orbit Earth.
New: K-Mart and WalMart stores opened.

1963: The Post Office introduced ZIP codes.
Federal legislation required "equal pay for equal work."
Dr. Martin Luther King, Jr. gave his "I Have a Dream" speech.
President Kennedy assassinated in Dallas, Texas.
New: 1963: pop top cans.

1963–1969 U.S. President Lyndon B. Johnson.

1964: The Wilderness Act sets aside area "where earth and its community of life are untrammeled by man."
Martin Luther King, Jr. won the Nobel Peace Prize.
New: Ford Mustangs; Jeopardy game show.

1965: President Johnson increased the draft to 35,000 a month.
New: Gatorade.

1966: Nearly 400,000 U.S. troops in Southeast Asia.
New: "Star Trek" show; Operation game; Battleship game; Pampers disposable diapers.

1967: Dr. Christian Barnard: first successful heart transplant.
New: Daylight Savings Time; superballs; home microwave ovens.

1968: Assassination of Martin Luther King, Jr. in Memphis.
Shirley Chisholm: first black woman elected to Congress.
New: Spirograph; 60 Minutes.

1969: ***New:*** Hot Wheels; Sesame Street show; ATM machines.

1. In 1962 and 1963 the Supreme Court ruled that prayer and reading from the Bible in public schools was unconstitutional. What is your opinion about these two decisions?

____

____

2. The Supreme Court passed the Miranda Decision giving individuals accused of crimes the right to remain silent because ". . . anything you say, can and will be used against you in a court of law." What is your opinion of this decision?

____

____

Name ______________________________

Changes and Challenges

The sixties became a youth-centered decade as millions of "baby-boomers" grew up. The conservative fifties gave way to social change in values, lifestyles, fashions, law, and entertainment.

College students spoke out against the war in Vietnam and racial and sexual discrimination. They supported individual freedom, new values, and a new lifestyle. Many young people turned to mystic eastern beliefs. Respect for authority declined; crime rates and drug use soared.

People sang to folk music and danced to rock 'n roll. Dance crazes included the Twist, the Mashed Potato, the Swim, the Watusi, the Monkey, and the Jerk. The Beatles and other British rock groups topped the music charts. Elvis Presley remained popular for the entire decade. The musical phenomenon of the decade was Woodstock, a three-day music festival that drew 400,000 participants and featured peace, love, happiness, and music.

The Russians led the space race, but the U.S. wasn't far behind. The first Russian astronaut, Yuri Gagarin, orbited Earth in 1961. Less than a month later, U.S. astronaut Alan Shepard went into space aboard **Freedom 7**.

The race didn't run smoothly, however. In 1962 an unmanned spaceship launched to provide the first close-up view of Venus crashed four minutes after take-off. Three American astronauts scheduled to make the first trip to the moon in 1967 on **Apollo 1** died during a routine test. Oxygen in the capsule burst into flames killing Ed White, Gus Grissom, and Roger Chaffee.

Four days later two more American astronauts died in a fire in a flight simulator. NASA canceled all flights until December 1968, when **Apollo 8** carried three men into orbit around the moon and back to Earth.

The goal of the sixties was to be the first to land astronauts on the moon—and bring them back safely. On July 20, 1969 after orbiting the moon, Neil Armstrong and "Buzz" Aldrin landed the lunar module **Eagle** on the surface of the moon.

About 600 million people saw Neil Armstrong become the first person to walk on the moon and heard his famous words: "That's one small step for a man, a giant leap for mankind."

1. Listen to several Number 1 hit songs of the 1960s. On another sheet of paper, compare those songs to today's top hits.
2. On another sheet of paper, explain what you think Neil Armstrong meant when he said, "That's one small step for man, a giant leap for mankind."

Name ______________________________

Civil Rights

The Civil Rights movement of the sixties began with Martin Luther King, Jr. leading sit-ins and peaceful protests. Over 200,000 peaceful demonstrators joined King and other leaders in 1963 in a March on Washington D.C. to support passage of Civil Rights laws. Although segregation in schools was illegal, the University of Mississippi tried to prevent James Meredith, a black student, from enrolling in 1962. He filed suit and a federal court ordered desegregation of the university. The governor of Mississippi tried to intervene. President Kennedy sent federal marshals to accompany Meredith. Riots broke out on campus.

When the governor of Alabama tried to block desegregation at the University of Alabama, Kennedy sent U.S. soldiers to enforce the law and prevent riots.

Kennedy proposed several Civil Rights laws, but was assassinated before they could be passed. President Johnson told Congress: ". . . all of us must . . . overcome the crippling legacy of bigotry and injustice. And . . . we . . . shall . . . overcome."

Congress passed the Civil Rights Act of 1964 which prohibited segregation and racial discrimination in public accommodations, government-owned facilities, education, and employment. A year later the Voting Rights Act of 1965 eliminated literacy tests and poll taxes as conditions for voting.

The assassination of Martin Luther King, Jr. on April 4, 1968 touched off riots in Washington, D.C. and other American cities.

The Civil Rights Act of 1968 made it illegal to discriminate in the sale or rental of housing or to prevent anyone from voting, working, attending school, performing jury duty, or participating in federally assisted programs.

1. What do you think about the governor of a state attempting to prevent a federal law from being enforced?

   ____

   ____

2. These laws made segregation and discrimination illegal, but they couldn't change reality immediately. Why do you think people continued to discriminate against others, even when it was illegal?

   ____

   ____

   ____

Name ______________________________

Timeline 1970–1979

1969–1973 U.S. President Richard M. Nixon

1970: U.S. population is 203,302,031.
First "Earth Day" celebrated.
Women were first promoted to generals in the U.S. Army.
Nixon announced invasion of Cambodia by American troops.
Four students killed during anti-war demonstration at Kent State University.

1971: Disney World opened in Orlando, Florida.
The 28th Amendment lowered the voting age from 21 to 18.
Huge anti-war march in Washington, D.C.

1972: The last U.S. combat ground forces were withdrawn from Vietnam.
Watergate scandal revealed.
Joanne Pierce and Susan Roley: first female FBI agents.
Alcatraz became a national park.
New: Pong, the first home video game.

1973: The Supreme Court legalized abortion.
Arab oil embargo caused energy prices to skyrocket.
New: UPC barcodes.

1974–1977 U.S. President Gerald R. Ford.

1974: President Nixon resigned.
President Ford granted Richard Nixon a full pardon.
The word "Internet" was first used.

1975: Two attempts to assassinate President Ford failed.
Lyme disease was first discovered.
Bill Gates and Paul Allen started Micro-Soft®.
New: mood rings; disposable razors; catalytic converters; pet rocks.

1977–1981 U.S. President Jimmy Carter.

1978: ***New:*** electronic typewriters.

1979: CompuServe went online.
The U.S. Mint began producing Susan B. Anthony dollars.
Hostages taken in Iran.
New: Sony Walkmans; cellular telephones.

1. OSHA became a new government agency. Use reference sources. What does OSHA stand for?

____

2. The EPA formed to establish standards to prevent and control pollution, toxic waste, and radioactive waste. Use reference sources. What does EPA stand for?

____

3. When the Sears Tower opened in 1973 it was the world's largest building. Use a reference source.

What city is it in? ____________________ How tall is it? ____________________

Name ______________________________

The Computer Age Begins

At the beginning of the 70s the U.S. remained deeply involved in the unpopular war in Southeast Asia. Anti-war protests continued. During this decade, Hispanic Americans and Native Americans struggled for equal rights. The Women's Rights Movement gained momentum. Although Congress approved the Equal Rights Amendment in 1972 to provide equal rights between men and women including equal pay for equal work, the Amendment failed to be approved in the required three-fourths of states and was not added to the Constitution.

Due to hijackings, screening of passengers and luggage became mandatory in 1972 on all U.S. domestic and foreign flights.

In 1975, Karen Ann Quinlin suffered severe, irreversible brain damage. After more than a year in a coma with no hope of improvement, her parents requested removal of artificial life support. The hospital refused. A New Jersey Supreme Court finally ruled that the device could be disconnected so the patient could "die with dignity." Although Karen never regained consciousness, she lived without life support until 1985.

One of the biggest changes of the decade came in electronics with the development of the silicon chip. Computers evolved from huge, room-size, expensive models to the first practical personal computers. The "computer age" began.

By 1973 a build-your-own computer kit cost $575. Two years later, IBM produced portable computers that weighed 50 pounds and cost $9,000 for only 16K of memory. The "deluxe" version, for a whopping $20,000, provided 64K of memory. (64K is less memory than the small hand-held video games available 10 years later for about $30.) 1,000K equals one megabyte. 1,000 megabytes equals one gigabyte. By the end of the century, people measured computer memory in gigabytes.

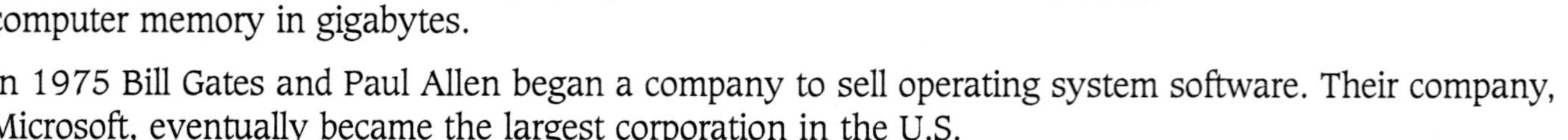

In 1975 Bill Gates and Paul Allen began a company to sell operating system software. Their company, Microsoft, eventually became the largest corporation in the U.S.

Steve Jobs and Steve Wozniak built the Apple I in a garage in 1976 and sold 600 units for $666.60. When they came out with the Apple II the following year, people bought them as fast as they could be built.

Further developments enabled smaller and more powerful computers to become available at less cost.

1. What do you think you would do if you had to make a decision like Karen Ann Quinlin's parents did? Write your answer on another sheet of paper.
2. On another sheet of paper, list five ways computers have affected our society.

Name ______________________________

Scandal in the White House

Richard Nixon, a Republican, became President in 1969. In June 1972 Republican agents burglarized Democratic headquarters at the Watergate Building Complex. Washington D.C. police arrested five men including James W. McCord, security chief for CREEP (Committee to Reelect the President). Police found telephone-tapping devices, cameras, walkie-talkies, burglary tools, and $4,500 in new hundred dollar bills in their hotel rooms.

Investigators found these men had secretly installed electronic listening devices to monitor Democratic campaign plans a month earlier. Two others were involved, but not caught until August: G. Gordon Liddy, legal financial advisor for CREEP and E. Howard Hunt, a White House consultant. President Nixon publicly denied any involvement "in this very bizarre incident."

In September 1972 a Washington grand jury charged the seven men with crimes related to the Watergate burglary. In spite of the scandal Richard Nixon was re-elected President in November.

Five men pleaded guilty to burglary, conspiracy, and illegal wiretapping. All seven were convicted and sentenced to prison. In April 1973 Nixon admitted ". . . there had been an effort to conceal the facts," and blamed his staff. He claimed no knowledge of events and complete innocence.

During public hearings that summer, one of the men claimed White House officials had covered up involvement in the scandal and pressured the defendants to plead guilty.

More illegal activities came to light. Nixon campaign workers had published lies to ruin the chances of some Democratic candidates. Contributions to Nixon's campaign had been accepted in exchange for promises of future favors. Unreported funds had been used to finance Watergate.

An investigating committee requested secret tapes Nixon had made of White House conversations. Under pressure, he finally released some tapes, but parts had been erased. For a time he refused to hand over 64 other tapes.

Faced with charges of extortion, tax evasion, and bribery for actions prior to becoming vice-president, Spiro Agnew pleaded no contest to income tax evasion and resigned in 1973. He was later fined and sentenced to three years probation.

The House Judiciary Committee voted to impeach Nixon. Rather than face an impeachment trial, Nixon resigned in August 1974.

On another sheet of paper, answer these questions.

1. Why do you think Watergate made people distrust politicians?
2. Why do you think Nixon was reelected in 1972?
3. Do you think it was right that Nixon received a full pardon?

Name ______________________________

Timeline 1980–1989

1980: U.S. population is 226,545,805.
Mount St. Helens erupted.
Voyager 1 sent back images of Saturn and its moons.
CNN began broadcasting 24 hour news.
Small pox considered eradicated by World Health Organization.
U.S. refused to attend Summer Olympics in Moscow, Russia*.
New: cordless telephones

1981–1989 U.S. President Ronald Reagan.

1981: President Ronald Reagan shot by John Hinckley.
MTV debuted on cable.
Sandra Day O'Connor: first female Supreme Court Justice.
52 American hostages released from Iran* after 14 months.
1982: Vietnam Memorial erected in Washington, D.C.
Tylenol scare/deaths.
1983: U.S. invaded Grenada*.
40 killed in bombing of U.S Embassy in Beirut, Lebanon*.
241 U.S. Marines killed in bombing in Beirut.
Sally Ride: first American woman in space.
Vanessa Williams: first black Miss America.
Jesse Jackson: first black presidential candidate.
1984: Soviets and allies boycotted Summer Olympics in Los Angeles.
AIDS virus discovered.
Geraldine Ferraro: first woman Vice-Presidential candidate.
New: portable CD players; 3½-inch computer disks.
1985: Leaded gas officially banned in U.S.
Titanic wreckage found and filmed by robotic camera.
Rock 'n' Roll Hall of Fame opened.
1986: Iran-Contra scandal reported.
Challenger exploded shortly after lift-off killing all crew.
Return of Haley's Comet.
U.S. military planes dropped bombs on Libya*.
Martin Luther King Jr.'s birthday became a legal holiday.
1987: Half of all U.S. homes with TV had cable.
World population reached 5 billion.
Coca-Cola became #1 soft drink, pushing Pepsi-Cola to #2.
1988: First transatlantic telephone calls over fiber optic lines.
U.S. invaded Panama*.
98% of U.S. homes had at least one television set.
Explosion of airplane over Lockerbie, Scotland, blamed on Libyan terrorists.
Music CDs outsold vinyl records.

1989–1993: U.S. President George H. Bush.

1989: **Voyager 2** sent back images of Neptune.
Exxon **Valdez** oil disaster in Alaska
Worldwide ban of ivory
Colin Powell appointed Chief of Staff of the Army, highest army post ever held by a black officer.
Earthquake postponed third game of the World Series.
Arsenio Hall: first black to host a nightly talk show.

On a world map, locate the countries marked with an *.

Name ______________________________

Reaganomics Dominated the Eighties

The presidency of Ronald Reagan dominated the eighties. His critics felt that his conservative economic policies favored big business and the wealthy. He reduced or ended many federal programs in order to cut government expenses and reduce taxes. By paying less taxes, he hoped people would spend more and the economy would improve.

Reagan also took a strong stand against terrorism. In 1983 he sent 800 U.S. soldiers to Lebanon as part of an international peacekeeping effort. He believed communism was a great evil that must be stopped. He also sent 1,900 U.S. soldiers to Grenada to prevent Cuba from establishing a communist government there.

In 1986 the public learned that high-ranking members of the Reagan administration had arranged for the secret sale of arms to Iran, in direct violation of current U.S. laws. Profits from the $30 million in weapon's sales were channeled to guerrilla forces fighting against the communist government in Nicaragua. An investigation concluded that although there was no evidence that Reagan had broken the law, the president may have participated in, or known about, a cover-up.

Fashions in the eighties went to extremes from the "grunge" look and punk styles of hair and clothing to the conservative suits and haircuts worn by yuppies (young urban professionals).

Advances in technology, especially personal computers, continued as PCs became more powerful. Laptop computers, solar-powered, hand-held calculators, music CDs, the point and click computer mouse, cell phones, camcorders, video games, and disposable cameras became available during the eighties.

Cable television introduced MTV, CNN, and home shopping networks. Malls sprang up across the country and the use of credit cards increased dramatically.

NASA's space shuttle program was very active until the space shuttle **Challenger** exploded killing everyone aboard 73 seconds after takeoff in January 1986. This delayed the program for two years until stricter controls could be put in place.

1. Why do you think the economy would improve if people spent more money?

   ____

   ____

   ____

2. What do you think? Does a president have a right to break a law, even if he feels it is for a "good cause?" Write your answer on another sheet of paper.

3. Use the Internet to find samples of the grunge look, punk style, and yuppie styles of clothing. On another sheet of paper, compare and contrast these styles. Give your opinion of each.

Name ____

Timeline 1990–1999

1990: U.S. population is 248,709,873.
Dr. Jack Kevorkian assisted patient suicide.
Hubble space telescope launched.
Clean Air Act passed.

1991: U.S. bombed Iraq: Persian Gulf War began.
New: Courtroom Television Network.

1992: Race riots in Los Angeles.

1993: Siege at Waco, Texas.
Combat roles became available for women in U.S. military.
Bombing of the World Trade Center in New York killed five.

1993–2001 U.S. President Bill Clinton.

1994: Amazon.com began selling books online.
Existence of black holes proved.
Massive earthquake in Los Angeles.

1995: Bombing at Oklahoma City federal building killed 168.
O.J. Simpson found not guilty of murder.
Sony demonstrated flat screen TV.
Major U.S. dailies created national online newspaper network.
Audio of live events available on the Internet.
Dr. Bernard A. Harris, Jr.: first black American astronaut to walk in space.

1996: U.S. athletes won 101 medals at Summer Olympics in Atlanta.
The Unabomber, Theodore Kaczynski, was arrested in Montana.
30 million Internet users in U.S.
Olympic Park bombing: two killed.
Truck bomb in Saudi Arabia killed 19 soldiers in barracks.
Flight 800 from New York crashed, killing all aboard.
New: Tickle Me Elmo.

1997: IBM computer defeated world chess champion Garry Kasparov.
AOL boasted 10 million subscribers.
43% of U.S. homes had computers.
New: Kodak point-and-shoot digital camera.
First successful clone of a mammal in Scotland.

1998: Impeachment trial of President Clinton.
Two young boys killed five at an Arkansas middle school.
New: colorful iMac computer.

1999: Senate acquitted President Clinton.
Shooting at Columbine High School resulted in 15 deaths.
Viruses continued to attack computers.
217 killed in Egypt Air crash off coast of Nantucket.
Control of Panama Canal given to Panama.
40 million American households on the Internet.
First non-stop around-the-world balloon trip.

1. Use reference sources. What animal was cloned? ____________________
2. If you could travel around the world in a hot air balloon, would you go? Why or why not? Write your answer on another sheet of paper.

Name ____

At the End of the Century

Americans became more aware of terrorism in the nineties with the bombing of the World Trade Center, the bombing of the Murrah Federal Building in Oklahoma City, and a series of shooting rampages in schools.

Before being captured in 1996, Theodore Kacynski killed three people and injured 29 others with homemade letter bombs. He believed technology would destroy the world and targeted people he considered a threat.

Episodes of racial violence during the nineties showed that in spite of progress, severe problems still existed.

On October 8, 1998 the House of Representatives voted to open an impeachment inquiry against President Clinton on charges of perjury and obstruction of justice. After a five-week trial, the Senate voted not guilty 55 to 45 on the first charge and 50 to 50 on the second one. Clinton remained President.

There was some good news, however. The nineties were a prosperous period for most Americans. Unemployment and inflation remained low for much of the decade.

While president, Clinton appointed more women and members of minorities to his Cabinet and other important positions. He signed the Family and Medical Leave Act making it illegal to fire someone for taking time off to care for an ill family member.

The constantly quickening pace of technological changes and widespread availability of the Internet allowed people with a computer to access data, read newspapers or magazines, and find financial, legal, or medical advice.

The Internet provided new ways to communicate through e-mail and chat rooms. Companies could advertise and sell on-line. Customers could compare products and order almost anything from a book to a new car. With more options for Internet shopping, banking, and paying, privacy and security became an important issue.

1. Use reference sources to learn more about why Clinton was impeached. Write a summary of what you learned on another sheet of paper.

2. List three ways you use computers. ____

____

____

3. How has the Internet affected your life? ____

____

____

Name ____

Nineties News

1. Use the Internet and other reference sources to learn more about one of these 1990s events.
2. Write a newspaper article summarizing the events and the consequences that resulted. Answer the questions who, what, when, where, why, and how in your article. Add an illustration.
3. Write a separate editorial expressing your opinion of the event.

Nineties News

- NASA launched the Hubble Space Telescope in 1990 at a cost of $1.5 million. Once in orbit, many problems developed.
- A coalition of 30 nations including the U.S. sent more than half a million troops to the Middle East in 1991.
- Four white police officers in Los Angeles were videotaped beating a black man, Rodney King, on March 3, 1991. When a court found the policemen not guilty in 1992, one of the worst race riots in U.S. history broke out.
- Members of the Branch Davidian cult living in a compound in Waco, Texas began shooting when federal officials tried to arrest their leader, David Koresh, for possession of illegal firearms on February 28, 1993. After a 51-day standoff, agents used tear gas and stormed the compound.
- President Clinton appointed his wife, Hillary, to head a commission to develop a plan to reform health care. In September 1993, the Clinton health care plan went to Congress for approval.
- A van packed with a 1,210-pound bomb exploded in the parking garage underneath the World Trade Center on February 26, 1993 killing six people, injuring more than a thousand, and trapping tens of thousands of workers.
- President Clinton signed the Brady Law which required a five-day waiting period for people purchasing handguns so background checks could be made.
- In 1995 Timothy McVeigh used a powerful truck bomb to blow up the Alfred P. Murrah Federal Building in Oklahoma City killing 168 men, women, and children.
- A raft carrying six-year-old Elian Gonzalez, his mother, step-father, and other Cuban refugees sank off the coast of Miami. After the boy was rescued, an international custody battle began.
- Two students went on a shooting rampage killing 12 students and one teacher before killing themselves on April 20, 1999 at Columbine High School in Littleton, Colorado.

Name ____________________________________

Twentieth Century Fun Facts

Collecting and trading picture postcards became a great fad in the 1910s. Postcards cost a penny.

Edwin George attached a gasoline washing machine motor to a hand-pushed lawn mower in 1919 and invented the power lawn mower.

In 1930 two men drove from New York to Los Angeles and back in 42 days. It wasn't the first or fastest transcontinental automobile trip, but it was the first time anyone did it driving backwards all the way!

Pinball machines were illegal in Atlanta, Georgia in 1939.

Mel Blanc, the voice for Bugs Bunny, was allergic to carrots. When sound effects called for munching carrots, Blanc crunched them, then spit them out.

Baseball legend Willie Mays struck out his first time at bat in the Major Leagues and also the next 26 times he stepped up to the plate. Then he improved and became the 1951 Rookie of the Year.

Bertha Diugi wanted her pet bird to fly around the house without making a mess. In 1956 she received a patent for bird diapers.

People watched the first Peanuts TV special, "A Charlie Brown Christmas" in 1965. A year later the dynamic duo of Batman and Robin came to television.

When John F. Kennedy was president, his daughter Caroline rode her pet pony on the White House lawn.

A major change in men's fashions took place in the mid-seventies with the introduction of high platform shoes and polyester "leisure suits" available in bright shades of purple, rose, orange, and lime green.

While testing the microphone before his weekly radio broadcast on August 10, 1984 President Reagan joked, "My fellow Americans, I am pleased to tell you that I just signed legislation that would outlaw Russia forever. We begin bombing in five minutes." Reagan didn't know his words were being broadcast.

President Reagan liked jelly beans. As governor and president, he always kept a jar of jelly beans on his desk.

In 1982 Larry Walters tied 42 weather balloons to a lawn chair and flew to 16,000 feet before shooting the balloons with a pellet gun. The FAA fined him $1,500.

Use reference sources to find three other "fun facts" about the twentieth century. Write them on 3" x 5" index cards. Combine your cards with your classmates' and arrange them in a timeline.

Name ___________________________

Learn More About . . .

Use reference sources to write a five to ten page report about one of these people who made an impact on the twentieth century.

Jane Addams
Madeleine Albright
Margaret Walker Alexander
Maya Angelou
Louis Armstrong
Alexander Graham Bell
Mary McLeod Bethune
Gwendolyn Brooks
Pearl S. Buck
Barbara Bush
George H. Bush
Richard E. Byrd
Jane Byrne
Dale Carnegie
Jimmy Carter
George Washington Carver
Cesar Chavez
Shirley Chisholm
Bill Clinton
Hillary Clinton
Calvin Coolidge
Douglas Coorigan
Charles E. Coughlin
Mildred Babe Didrickson
Walt Disney
W.E.B. DuBois
Amelia Earhart
Jocelyn Elders
Dwight D. Eisenhower
Duke Ellington
Edna Ferber
Geraldine Ferraro
Henry Ford
Betty Friedan
Bill Gates
John Glenn
William Harding
Penny Harrington
Herbert Hoover
Harry Houdini
Jesse Jackson
Dr. Mae C. Jemison
Lyndon B. Johnson
Mary Harris Jones
Florence Griffith Joyner
John F. Kennedy
Martin Luther King Jr.
Rodney King
Sinclair Lewis
Charles Lindbergh
Juliette Low
Malcolm X
Christa McAuliffe
Margaret Mead
Carrie Nation
Richard Nixon
Oliver North
Jesse Owens
Rosa Parks
Frances Perkins
Janet Reno
Nancy Reagan
Ronald Reagan
Sylvia Plath
Colin Powell
Jackie Robinson
John D. Rockefeller
Will Rogers
Eleanor Roosevelt
Franklin Roosevelt
Theodore Roosevelt
Nellie Taylor Ross
Florence Sabin
Carl Sandburg
Margaret Sanger
Norman Schwarzkopf
Dr. Seuss
Donna Shalala
Upton Sinclair
Gertrude Stein
John Steinbeck
Gloria Steinem
William Taft
Jim Thorpe
Harry S. Truman
George Wallace
Booker T. Washington
Woodrow Wilson
Frank Lloyd Wright
Orville Wright
Wilbur Wright
Chuck Yaeger

Name ____

Resources for Students

The Noble Experiment, 1919–1933 by James P. Barry

Ticket to the Twenties: A Time Traveler's Guide by Mary Blocksma

The Impeachment of William Jefferson Clinton by Daniel Cohen

The Great Depression by David Downing

Timelines: a series by Jane Duden and Gail Stewart

World War II: On the Homefront by Phyllis Emert

An Album of the Sixties by Carol A. Emmens

20th Century Pop Culture: The 60s; 20th Century Pop Culture: The 70s; 20th Century Pop Culture: the Early Years to 1949: by Dan Epstein

The 1940s: From World War II to Jackie Robinson; The 1950s: From the Korean War to Elvis; The 1960s: From the Vietnam War to Flower Power; The 1980s: From Ronald Reagan to MTV; The 1990s: From the Persian Golf War to Y2K by Stephen Feinsten

The Watergate Scandal in American History by David K. Fremon

A Look at Life in the Eighties by Adrian Gilbert

War, Peace, and All that Jazz by Joy Hakim

The Usborne History of the Twentieth Century by Christina Hopkinson

Kitty Hawk: Flight of the Wright Brothers by Karen Price Hossell

An Album of the Great Depression by William Loren Katz

America in the 1960s by Michael Kronenwetter

Life During the Great Depression by Dennis Nishi

The United States Since 1945 by Nigel Smith

The Roaring Twenties; The Great Depression; and The Assassination of John F. Kennedy by R. Conrad Stein

The 1930s: Picture History of the 20th Century by Richard Tames

The Cold War by David Taylor

The Vietnam War by Douglas Willoughby

Answer Key

Timeline 1900–1909, page 1
1. Atlantic and Pacific Oceans. This shortcut reduced sailing distance and time.

Life Was Different Then, page 2
1. Annual means per year.
2. $674.96 per year
3. 22 cents an hour

Timeline 1910–1919, page 3
1. 1876
2. Transcontinental means across the continent

The War to End All Wars, page 4
2. the right to vote

The Roar Before the Crash, page 6
1. dance marathon: a dance contest that continued until people were too exhausted to continue. The last couple standing won the contest.
2. They borrowed money and used their homes as collateral. The bank owned the home until the loan was repaid.
3. Illiteracy means the inability to read and write

The Great Depression of the 1930s, page 9
1. a period when prices and unemployment are high and money is scarce
2. Drought means a long period of time with little rain
3. four

Timeline 1940–1949, page 10
1. Internment means imprisonment.
2. The Gestapo was the Nazi German police.
3. to travel faster than the speed of sound

World War II Changed America, page 11
1. limitations on what and how much could be purchased
2. Union of Soviet Socialist Republic

Timeline 1950–1959, page 12
1. Segregation means separation because of race, religion, or sex
2. USSR/Sputnik I

Timeline 1970–1979, page 17
1. OSHA stands for Occupational Safety and Health Administration.
2. Environmental Protection Agency
3. Chicago/1454 feet tall

Timeline 1990–1999, page 22
1. a sheep